MUMS' A[...]

RATTLES & BATTLES

by Nicola Pitchers

Typeset by Jason Wightman
Illustrations by Paul Bale

Copyright © Nicola Pitchers 2016
All rights reserved

No part of this book may be reproduced, or stored in a retrieval system, or transmitted in any form or by any means, electronic, mechanical, photocopying, recording or otherwise, without express written permission of the publisher.

The contents of this book are the authors own thoughts and opinions. It is not intended or implied to be a substitute for professional medical advice. Always seek the advice of your GP, midwife or other qualified health provider with any concerns.

CONTENTS

Introduction 1

Chapter One: Preconceptions 7

Chapter Two: Birth (In hospital and coming home) 11

Chapter Three: First Few Weeks 19

Chapter Four: Crying 27

Chapter Five: Sleep (or lack of it) 35

Chapter Six: Body/Self Image 41

Chapter Seven: Sex/Communication with Partner 47

Chapter Eight: Comparing Yourself with Others and Going Out 55

Chapter Nine: Guilt and Worry 59

Chapter Ten: See the Funny Side 65

Conclusion 69

A Final Thought 71

INTRODUCTION

I love children, I love being around them. I love the way they see the world.

From the age of about 12, I was the neighbourhood baby-sitter. I loved their company, I loved playing silly games and acting the clown. It was always great fun having crazy adventures and getting lost in a child's world of imagination and play.

Everyone would tell me I was a 'natural' and that if I had my own children one day, I'd be a great mum.

So, I had always imagined if I did have my own children, I would love everything about it. I would daydream about the fun things we would do, and the adventures we would have of our own. I would think about all the things I'd like to teach them, knowing right from wrong, seeing their amazement at the world and hopefully help them to be well rounded, confident, happy and healthy individuals.

However, what I hadn't factored into my dream scenario of my idyllic future life with my idyllic children, was that before you could have the 'fun' and the 'adventures', they had to be babies first!!

Nothing could have prepared me on my road to becoming a mother of what it was like to have BABIES!!!!

They can't understand what I'm saying, they can't get themselves up and dressed and jump in the car ready to go exploring in the forest and have an adventure. They can't help me make chocolate cookies and lick all the goo off the spoon. They can't go to the toilet on their own to do their business and wash their hands afterwards. They can't laugh at my silly jokes or play hide and seek around the garden?

What they can do is scream, vomit, scream, poo, scream, get hot, scream and if you're lucky sometimes they sleep.

Why did I not think about what having babies was like?!

I didn't realise I would be about to experience a whole new life and a big chunk of baby reality full of RATTLES AND BATTLES!

After going through the dreaded baby stage with my first child, and then - as all parents seem to - suffering from 'baby stage amnesia', I found myself plunged head first, back into newborn madness with my second 18 months later…and everything just came flooding back.

So, when my friend asked me to tell her honestly what it was like to have a baby and be a first-time mum, I thought - I must write a few things down for her before it is all forgotten. As everyone knows all the good stuff, people are more than quick to tell you all those bits. The cuddles, the gorgeous baby smell, the wonder of staring at a sleeping newborn blah blah blah. However, the not so good bits they don't tell you about! And let's face it, they are the bits we want to know and prepare ourselves for!

I always remember when I first plucked up the courage to say to my sister that I sometimes felt like I didn't want to look after my baby all day and that sometimes when he was screaming I felt angry towards him. I was worried that she would think I was a crap mum or something but she just turned round and said 'Oh yeah that's normal! I hated having a baby sometimes too and it used to send me crazy when she wouldn't stop screaming' I couldn't believe it!! 'Why didn't you tell me all this?' and like most of us she just said 'Well I'd forgotten it all and you don't really talk about that side of things'.

With that in mind, if you then experience anything of the same, you won't be too upset and shocked by it, you will actually realise it is quite normal. What is it they say…

Forewarned is forearmed?

Therefore, before my 'baby stage amnesia' kicks in, and I start telling people how much I loved it when my children were babies, how good they were, how I can't remember them crying much, I thought I would give a few words of insight to people who may be starting their own journey on the road to parenthood. Or for someone who is supporting a soon to be parent, partner, friend, relative and anyone who might like a heads-up of what the feelings and thoughts a new mum might possibly have (the ones that are not always that positive) in the first six months or so of having a baby.

I know we all have different family situations - some people are single parents, some people do not have any relatives around them, and I can only speak from my own experiences - so not everything in this book may ring true with you, but hopefully you will be able to relate to some parts of it and have a bit of a giggle too. It is not about highlighting our differences, it is more about realising our similarities to one another and standing together to support each other during this scary new uncharted territory we are about to dive head first into.

Everyone is aware of how wonderful and amazing it can be to have a baby. Just look on your social media accounts, where parents proudly display their gorgeous smiling babies to all and sundry proclaiming their love, and sharing with the world all their happy moments. We have all seen the magazine and television interviews with people in the public eye proclaiming to have found the reason why they have been put on this Earth, and how having a baby has enriched their lives etc. - and all that is fantastic. It is lovely to hear happy stories for a change and it fills you with positivity.

This book is not about that side of motherhood, it is about the other side. The side that is not put on social media and isn't discussed as often, but it is a side that you need to be aware of so it gives you a true perspective of the question. 'What is it like to have a baby and be a first time mum'?

Many conversations with my family and close friends made me realise that, to some degree, we all pretty much felt the same way when our children were babies (even my mum admitted she did not always like me and my sister much when we were babies). This was a huge comfort when I thought it was just me who sometimes wanted to tear my hair out. I was lucky, because I had friends who were having or just had babies at the same time as me, so we spoke about things quite openly and honestly and, knowing they were struggling just like I was, gave me a massive sense of relief.

However, even with an extremely supportive partner, great family and brilliant friends there were still times when I felt incredibly alone, overwhelmed and in fear of my own sanity - so goodness knows what it must be like for people who do not have that support network around them. So I hope these words comfort you if you have a 'wobble' moment and reassure you that by no means are you alone.

However, you might find that nothing in this book relates to you at all, as all you felt was pure joy from the moment your baby was born and not one negative thought engulfed you at any time. If that's the case then I am genuinely happy for you, and extremely jealous and amazed and would urge you to write a book spilling your secrets!

For the rest of us, I think every mother needs an army behind them....

Let's all fall in….

Mums' Army

Chapter One

PRECONCEPTIONS

'We're gonna need a bigger boat'

Well, my dearest friend, you asked me for an honest account of what it feels like to have a baby from a mother's point of view. Well, let me tell you some things you may or may not experience from day zero to twelve months of life with your gorgeous new baby.

Like me, I know you enjoy the odd bit of celebrity gossip and a reality show now and again. We read magazine articles and watch television interviews of people in the public eye having their babies - and how much 'joy' and 'happiness' it has brought them. How their lives are now fulfilled and complete, and they are looking all glamorous and svelte in the seven page spread, with their gorgeous smiling newborns dressed as fairies or elves.

They tell us how easy they have found motherhood, how breastfeeding was a moving, humbling spiritual experience, and how the baby weight just 'fell off' from running around so much after their babies (still don't get that one, a baby doesn't move!? Where are they all running to?).

We might see our 'friends' on social media, always posting wonderful snapshots of their little cute babies and going on about how much they are 'in love' with them and how 'perfect' their lives are now.

The breastfeeding selfies with #borntobeamother. Everyone is so happy and they are all laughing and jolly, it gives a great impression that having babies is going to be a piece of cake, they fit into your life and bring you closer together with your partner. So it's completely natural to think we will be exactly the same, we will feel what they feel - right?

Well, you know what, motherhood is amazing and fantastic and wonderful and they are all totally right! However what they might not post or be as quick to tell you, is the other side of the coin. The not so amazing, fantastic and wonderful things that come along with motherhood the moment that little baby arrives into your world?

You may think, due to what you have seen that when your baby arrives you will feel happy all the time, closer with your partner, truly loved, and finally be able to understand the meaning of life, and a reason as to why you were put on this earth…. I'm sorry to tell you that this may not be the case.

You can have the most supportive partner, family or friends but it won't always stop you from sometimes feeling alone in those first few months and feeling completely overwhelmed.

Try not to let preconceptions and the idea of parenting cloud your mind too much, so that it doesn't allow the possibility that reality may be slightly different to what you are hoping or even expecting. There is nothing worse than building yourself up to something that you imagine is going to be a dream come true, to then come crashing down with a very large bump when it isn't quite as you imagined or were led to believe it would be (like watching the 'Fifty Shades of Grey' movie?).

For example, you may like me, whilst on maternity leave, write down a list of what you would like to achieve when you have 'time off'. This list may include various things such as:-

1. Write a book
2. Read a book
3. Lose the baby weight
4. Sort out my wardrobe
5. Watch 'Desperate Housewives' on box set
6. Go for a walk every day
7. Take baby to lots of classes
8. Do pelvic floor exercises every day
9. Go swimming every week
10. Put all my photos in albums
11. Do lots of baking
12. Learn baby sign language

This list you will swiftly find slightly off the mark (just slightly), as when you actually have the baby your list will become a teensy bit less ambitious such as:-

1. Get out of bed
2. Look after baby
3. Go back to bed

Let's start from the beginning…

Chapter Two

BIRTH (IN HOSPITAL AND COMING HOME)

'Please don't do a poo'

As soon as you are pregnant, people will be queueing up to tell you their birthing stories. Some of them will be fascinating, some of them will be harrowing, some of them will be funny and some of them will put the fear of God into you! Every single person that has given birth will have a slightly different tale to tell.

You will listen and 'Oooh' 'Arghh' 'Eerrr' at all the gory details. You will also no doubt watch at least one episode of 'One Born Every Minute' or similar show, and excitedly spend time writing a birth plan. However, nothing will prepare you for what will be your own birthing story.

My mother's favourite saying when I was heavily pregnant and starting to experience 'birth fear' was always - 'Well, if it hurt that much, no-one would have more than one!'

Well, Mum, it did hurt that much! It was the most pain I have ever experienced. (Definitely more painful than when I dislocated my knee)

It can be a very worrying time the closer you get to your due date and there will no doubt be lots of thoughts going through your mind, which may include:-

1. Will I poo myself?
2. Is it possible to die from pain?
3. Will they think my vagina is weird or different to anyone else's
4. Should I shave all my pubic hair off?
5. Will I push out a pile?
6. Will they laugh at my piles?
7. Will there be lots of people seeing me naked?
8. Will I smell?

After birth your first thought may only be:-

1. How long before my tea and toast arrives?

It is totally true what everyone told me, my biggest fear of pooing on the midwife will totally pale into insignificance when I'm in labour, and I wont give a monkey's who sees me naked. Line up anyone from my class at high school and let them take a selfie with my piles because all I care about is getting my baby out!

No doubt your birthing experience will not have lived up to your expectations and it will not happen the way you had planned it in your head, but you got through it! That will be the main thing to focus on.

I was watching an interview with someone who said she felt a failure for having to have an epidural. Her plan was not to have anything except gas and air, and she was thoroughly disappointed in herself that she had to have drugs to help with the pain. That struck a worrying chord in my mind that she felt like that. How could anyone feel a failure after just giving birth?! You have carried a baby all that time, gone through all the woes of being pregnant (and there are a lot of woes) you have made life inside your body and that life has come into the world in whatever way possible… and you are going to start beating yourself up that you had to have some pain relief?! Is that just a woman thing? It would be interesting to hear what her partner had to say about it? Did he think she was a failure? Somehow I doubt it very much!

There are without doubt few greater moments than when your baby is first put into your arms. It is absolutely amazing. (Mainly when you think that you had something that huge in your stomach! How did it fit?)

Some people will say that is when you feel a huge sudden rush of love and completely fall in love with your little bundle. Will this be the case for you?

I'm not entirely convinced. My first thoughts were more of a primal instinct of protection. Feeling like you would give your life for this little bundle of pink flesh and gloop screaming on your chest. I remember feeling a huge sense of responsibility, thinking if anyone tries to hurt my baby they'll have to go through me first - literally! I wanted to protect him, that was the overwhelming feeling. I did not feel - 'Oh I love you so much' as you have only just met and surely love is an emotion that grows with time? So, if you don't feel that you instantly love this little baby, make sure you don't panic! That's quite a normal feeling, one that will change as time moves on. YOU'VE JUST HAD A BABY! Your hormones are having an all night rave! So try not to think too deeply about anything just yet.

Thoughts, feelings and emotions are all over the place after giving birth.

Straight after birth you may think you will feel:-
1. Elated
2. Totally in love with your baby
3. Your life is complete
4. Instantly closer to your partner
5. A natural mother and everything comes instinctively to you
6. A heroine

Don't be too upset if you feel:-
1. Total relief its over
2. A bit traumatised
3. Exhausted
4. Disappointed at how things went
5. Guilty you can't or don't want to breastfeed

6. Anxious
7. Overwhelmed
8. Frightened
9. Dreading when you need a poo
10. Sudden and complete feeling of huge responsibility

There is help available if you feel traumatised by your birth, I think a lot of mums do struggle to come to terms with how their birth went, and you don't hear much about that side of things. You're just expected to get on with looking after your baby, but you might feel really upset and confused about how things went and just need to talk it through with someone. You may have had a terribly horrific birth and need counselling about it. The midwives at the hospital can go through your birth with you and tell you a break down of everything that happened if you felt you needed to do that.

I think one of the worst things is when your partner is booted out and you have to be alone with your baby for the first time. You want to scream 'Don't go!', 'Don't leave me alone, I don't know what I'm doing!' It can be frightening and upsetting when you have to say goodbye and be wheeled through to the ward with all the other mums! You have no idea what to expect and feel totally out of your comfort zone.

There can be a feeling of immense fear when the midwife leaves you alone and inside you think - 'Stay with me and tell me what to do', 'I don't want to be on my own' - but there you are wheeled into the ward with all the other mums and babies and that's it, you're on your own with your baby and your thoughts, and its all down to you! #Panic

With your baby by your side in hospital once everything has calmed down and you have a moment to compose your thoughts, you imagine just staring into your baby's face and feeling on cloud nine. You kind of do, I remember just staring at his tiny little face, amazed by his skin and perfect features and little tiny hands and the tiny hairs on his cheek. However, I also felt scared, lonely, sore and guilty I could not breastfeed. I was petrified of when I would need the toilet, I felt nervous and stressed every time the baby moved or made a noise. And when he woke about 3am and was sick I think I nearly had a heart attack, pressing that nurse button frantically! I had a sudden sense of what a huge responsibility I now had on my shoulders, an actual human life in my hands. Not just any life, the life of something so precious that the weight and worry of that fact made me start to feel incredibly anxious. You'll be lucky if you get any sleep at all that first night.

You may lay in that hospital bed reliving how the birth went, thinking how on Earth are you going to cope looking after something that seems so fragile and didn't come with an instruction manual? Just getting through that first night alone in hospital can be a bit of an ordeal. I was counting the hours until my partner could come back in the morning, and was full of questions that I dare not ask anyone about, for fear of sounding stupid.

Can I wipe my bits after a wee or should I drip dry?

Where do I leave my baby when I go to the toilet? Do I take him with me?

Why does my belly feel like a water bed?

I've forgotten how to change a nappy, which bit is the front?

Will I break his arm trying to get it into this vest?

Are the other mums in this ward thinking I'm crap because my baby's crying?

They told me to use a bowl and water to wipe his bum, will they tell me off if they see me using a wet wipe?

Can I still remember the first aid training I had on that course?

Can I plug my phone charger into the wall?

When can I go home?

You will probably feel in two minds about leaving hospital, part of you will be relieved to be going back to your own home, your own surroundings, being with family, getting to have a nice bath and being in your own toilet. You may be glad to get away from all the eyes you feel are watching you and monitoring how you are looking after your baby. However, you may also feel nervous about leaving a healthcare facility! This is where all the midwives, doctors and nurses are on tap in case something happens. So it can be quite scary when they discharge you literally within what seems like a few hours of having your baby.

You will be so excited about getting your baby home you would have imagined this moment a lot. However, once you arrive and get settled in and put the baby on the floor peacefully asleep in the car seat, your first thought may be - 'Well, what do we do with him/her now?'

It's like you are on tenterhooks waiting for them to wake up, you can't quite relax, neither you or your partner want to be alone with the baby in case something happens. You are still in the new baby bubble where you can't quite believe what has happened in the last 24/48 hours - it all still seems like a dream.

You are in a state of shock and it will not really sink in that you are actually a parent now and after all that time your baby is finally here!

Many emotions will be hitting you about now - happiness, amazement, fear, confusion, relief, gratitude, just to name a few! It's going to be the start of a very emotional roller-coaster, so be prepared for the most thrilling ride of your life!

Chapter Three

FIRST FEW WEEKS

'We should have got a dog!'

To start with, you are in the 'baby bubble' and nothing has really hit you that much yet, as its just like being on holiday. The crying and the lack of sleep is like a temporary thing that you can quite perfectly handle. It is not until after about ten days into a holiday that you start to miss home a bit and get a bit bored, thinking that two weeks is definitely too long. Next time we will just go for a week, or ten days!

Once you start to get into week three or four of motherhood, you may experience some feelings and thoughts like:-

We've made a huge mistake

Regret at having a baby

Panicking about having such a huge responsibility on your shoulders

I can't do this

Mourning your previous life

Sick of worrying and feeling anxious all the time

Feel like you can't cope with the screaming

Feeling completely sleep deprived

Doubting everything you are doing

Googling everything

Snappy and irritable towards your partner

Feeling teary most days

Not feeling you will get through the day

Not realising how hard it was going to be

Feeling like your life how you knew it is over

Worrying you are doing everything wrong

Still not coming to terms with the actual birth

Paranoid at every spot or mark that appears on baby

The realisation of just how HUGE it is to have a baby

However, what you will probably say to your loved ones and to the world is - 'Yes, everything's fine'. You feel like you can't possibly complain about anything relating to your new life with your beautiful, healthy and longed-for baby. It is almost like you suppress any negative thoughts because you feel so grateful for being a mother, when so many people struggle to even conceive. Or the heartbreaking stories you read about babies, meaning it just feels wrong to voice any concerns or issues that are not the usual gushing sound bites most new mothers give about their babies - for fear of sounding ungrateful, mean, 'un-motherly' etc. While there are terrible stories that people have around conception, pregnancy and motherhood, you still have the right to speak openly and honestly about how you are feeling to your loved ones and friends. If you keep it all inside and try to deal with it on your own, it could lead to more serious issues down the line. When you start talking to people truthfully about things, you may be reassured when they tell you their truthful feelings about their experiences as well.

I think the biggest thing about having your first baby is coming to terms with the loss of your life as you knew it. You may be having your first child in your teens, twenties, thirties, forties - you were an independent woman, with your own identity, you may have liked certain sports, watching movies, socialising with friends, spending time as a couple, eating out, answering emails and texts, going on holidays, keeping fit. You had hobbies, you enjoyed 'me' time... and then suddenly overnight you have realised you feel a bit like a slave to your baby.

You might be thinking – 'Well that's a bit harsh! Or you might be thinking - 'Yep!' You might also think you would only feel like that if you are suffering from post-natal depression. Nope! That's a whole other thing, these feelings that have been familiar to me and lots of other mums are standard and normal feelings that most mums seem to feel at one point or another. However, they are temporary and they will disappear.

In those early months it can feel like all you are doing is just functioning.

You can't just 'nip' or 'pop' to the shop. 'Nipping' and 'popping' don't exist once you have children. You can't instantly respond to messages any more - if someone texts you, it's usually right in the middle of feeding time, then by the time you've changed nappies and wiped the projectile vomit from your clothes, you completely forgot someone sent you a message at all... and you reply about a week on Tuesday. Even having a shower or doing a poo becomes stressful. You can bet your life that, as soon as you step under that water or sit your bum down on the porcelain, the baby will decide to have a screaming fit and you move like a racing whippet to get to them.

You may have told yourself that life was going to be different once your baby arrives, and you are aware that you will not be able to do certain things like you did before children. Plus, a lot of the things you won't want to do anyway because you want to be with your baby. However, it's hard to experience the feelings until you actually experience them (if you know what I mean). I knew my life was going to change a lot, but it was still a shock by how much of a change it would be.

I never realised until I had a baby how much of a control freak I was. Now, I was no longer in control of any aspect of my life, it was like the baby had complete control over me, and with one cry would make me come running and drop everything. Not being able to do what I wanted when I wanted was actually a big deal for me to get my head around. You just have to learn to accept your new life and that does take time, it's not a 'quick' thing, I mean you may have had nearly forty years of it!

I did a lot better once I realised this, and I trained my brain to accept these things and just embraced the fact that I could not do things when I wanted to any more - and that if I did anything other than looking after my baby in the day (i.e. a bit of cleaning, or reply to an email) then that was a bonus!

I don't know if it is a woman thing, we try and do 'everything', but when you have a baby doing everything just isn't possible! We need to give ourselves a break and just accept that we can only do what we can, instead of heaping loads of pressure on ourselves.

Another wonderful thing to get your head around will be the screaming and sleepless nights. You'll never have previously been in a situation where day in day out you hear constant baby screams whilst being sleep deprived (unless you're a night nanny) so there is no way you can prepare your mind or body for this onslaught.

You may also feel as though you have gone from being a confident person into becoming a person who doesn't have a clue about anything any more!

Are we doing the bottles right?

If breastfeeding, are they taking enough?

Should we be bathing the baby more than three times a week?

Are we doing the right routine?

Will we ever be able to watch a TV show all the way to the end again?

Why does the baby projectile vomit over me all the time?

How will I cope when my partner goes back to work?

Am I sterilising properly?

Is baby's temperature okay?

How long should I let baby cry for?

Will I ever want to have sex again?

What does my vagina look like?

Why do I look like the Michelin man?

Why am I crying all the time?

Why can't I tell my partner how I'm feeling?

How can I cope with this lack of sleep?

Do I have to leave the house?

One of the things you may experience that will probably surprise you, are the feelings of frustration and even anger you may have towards the baby. You may find yourself shouting and screaming at your baby when they have a crying fit. Does this make you a bad mum? Is it normal?

Well, after chatting to other mums who have been through it, and googling 'Is it normal to feel anger towards your baby', I realised that it was common and quite normal to feel that way sometimes. I was not a bad mum! However, it is not something that is widely admitted to or discussed, I suppose through fear what people may think of you?

Give yourself a break, you have endured nine months of pregnancy, given birth from which you are still slightly traumatised, your hormones are all over the place, the whole family dynamic has changed, and you are now facing the huge responsibility of having another person's life in your hands. You are listening to a screaming baby for quite a few hours in the day, as well as having very little or no sleep every night! It is a massive thing! So of course your emotions and thoughts are going to be all over the place. I think most mums would admit they have held their screaming babies in their hands and just screamed back at them - 'What the **** is the matter with you?!' Or is that just me?

We are all told the basics about baby blues, but I don't think we are really told enough about the most common negative feelings you may experience. I think that's why it is important to get all sides of how it really feels to become a mum for the first time (not just the good stuff) from other mums that have been through it, so that you know if you have a few negative thoughts it doesn't automatically mean you must be doing something wrong or are abnormal!

I think baby blues are just coming to terms with this huge life changing event and there will be lots of tears, anger, frustration. I know with my first child I cried at some point each week for ten weeks. I was not suffering from post natal depression, it was just normal feelings that most parents go through and I was lucky enough to have honest new mums around me who spoke about how they felt - which made me realise being a mum wasn't just about all the wonderful stuff. There was actually some dark stuff as well to deal with. If you also feel like this, please take comfort in the fact you are normal and these feelings will pass.

However, if you feel that you could be suffering from something more, and that it could be post natal depression, please do not hesitate in getting help. They say that if you find yourself feeling down ALL the time and not taking pleasure in anything that you used to do before, you should speak to your GP, midwife or health visitor.

I knew I wasn't suffering from post natal depression as I still took great pleasure in a lot of things I used to do - like eating cake, watching guilty pleasure reality shows and drinking rose wine! So you will know in yourself if these feelings of despair are more than just baby blues, and there will be lots of help available to you.

I think sometimes because everyone's public stance is how wonderful motherhood is, and how in love with everything we are, that not many people talk openly about the negative side of parenting. It can sometimes come as a bit of a shock when you become a parent yourself, and you feel unprepared for these feelings. From only being aware of the 'good stuff', you feel like you are the only one in turmoil, and there must be something wrong with you. I think if we all spoke about the other side more often, people would realise that it is normal, and go into motherhood with a more well rounded true idea of what was possibly going to happen.

I don't think social media helps with this, as you only see the happy face of parenting, where everyone's smiling and having such a lovely time, you don't see the tantrums and tears that happened before or after, no-one goes on and says 'I really hate being a mother today' and 'my children are being evil monsters today' - we only tell people the good stuff.

So those first couple of months will be you and your loved ones adjusting to having a baby in your life. They will be full of ups and downs, your body is still recovering from giving birth and your hormones will still be all over the place. You may still be suffering from conditions relating to giving birth and you may be struggling with new routines and a new way of life. It's a hard bloody slog!

You may also, like me, be starting to mark in your diary the days until you get to the holy grail of twelve weeks…Why? Because that's when all the professionals, midwives, doctors and health visitors tell you the crying should die down by then……. read on!

Chapter Four

CRYING

Baby screaming = Sobbing mother

Well I'm sorry to tell you, but this topic needed a chapter all to itself. Your baby is going to cry! A lot!

Everyone has heard a baby screaming at some point in their lives, usually in a supermarket or a restaurant and you probably never gave it much thought.

Before children, when you heard a baby screaming you may have just thought - 'God, shut that baby up!'

After children, when you hear a baby screaming you just think 'Thank God that's not me! That poor woman!'

Unfortunately, nothing can prepare you for your own baby's screaming fits. My mother used to say that some of my music in my teenage years used to grate on her brain. I feel this is a perfect analogy for describing a baby's screams and how they make you feel. Literally get a cheese grater and rub it up and down a million times against your brain! (seriously, don't do that)

But hey, you never know, you might get lucky and get one of those babies that don't cry?

You know the ones! The ones you read about in magazine interviews and reality shows, where they tell you that their babies are amazing and that they never cry? I remember seeing one interview on telly, with a huge American country star, when I was in about week four of newborn baby madness. Along with telling the host how fantastic her life was now, what joy her baby had brought her, and what unbelievable love she felt - she said her baby NEVER cries, she is so GOOD! Err? Well does that mean that because my baby cries ALL The time he is BAD?

I thought crying was supposed to happen with babies? It was their only way of communicating, so surely if a baby isn't crying it's not a good thing? It would be an unusual thing? The baby is going against everything it's suppose to be programmed to do?

I think at this point I probably threw something at the telly!

Then there was the article where another mother said she could 'count on one hand the amount of times her baby had cried'?! What, in an hour? When did it become a shameful thing to admit that your baby cries? And cries a lot? Have these people not heard the nursery rhyme 'Wheels on the bus'? What did the babies do? Did they sit quietly in their mums' laps coo-ing and smiling? No, they were going 'Waaaah! Waaaah! Waaaah' 'cause that's what they do on the bus! And at home, and in the supermarket, and in their pram, and the car seat, and in their Moses basket at night at 2.30am!

So, if these mothers are telling the truth and I am sure they are, then that's great - but wouldn't it be wonderful if more mums who had experienced a screaming baby day and night would actually come out and say - 'You know what, my baby screams and screams and screams and it gets me so frustrated and down, and it's been a real battle these first few months!' Wouldn't we all feel so much respect, admiration and relief that someone was saying exactly what we felt as well? I think sometimes we need to just say it like it is. Like my nanny used to say…you can't polish a turd!

If you do happen to get one that cries you may find it all quite upsetting and distressing. I would assume, like me, you will at some point Google some things.

Is it normal for babies to cry so much?
Why do babies scream?
Can crying hurt a baby?
When does a baby stop crying so much?
How can I stop my baby from crying?
Is it my fault my baby is crying a lot?

You will go through it all - hungry, thirsty, tired, dirty, teething, pain, tight nappy, sock on the wrong way, doesn't like my choice of lipstick today. Sometimes a baby just wants to cry because it does! I liken it to… sometimes I just want to feel miserable and eat a large amount of cake! Just because I do!

I remember taking my first born to the doctors asking - is it a milk allergy, is it reflux, is it the formula, is it because I'm not warming the bottles, is it because my left ear is slightly bigger than my right ear, blah blah blah and he recites the line that he has no doubt given to a hundred mothers that week… 'It is probably just a bit of colic and the only thing really is time. When he gets to twelve weeks it will all settle down'.

I just cried all the way home and started a calendar counting down to the holy grail when this elusive twelve weeks would arrive, and duly ticked off each painstakingly long day after another.

It can be the most frustrating sound any parent can hear, and not being able to stop it becomes unbearable sometimes.

Are we doing something wrong?
Why don't they stop after we've checked everything?
Why is it our baby screams all the time and everyone else's seem to be fine?
Why is it when 6pm comes around he suddenly starts for no reason and carries on until 9pm!?

What I found most annoying was I kept needing a reason, there must be some reason why this baby is screaming! But I couldn't find one, they're not teething, hungry, thirsty, tired, they didn't have a tight nappy on, they didn't want cuddles, they just wanted to scream for apparently no reason at all - and scream in the early evenings for a few hours just when I want to have my tea!

Things got a lot better when I stopped trying to find a reason, and just accepted that it's something all babies have to do, over time it will stop, and I had to try and keep focusing on the fact that it wouldn't be forever, and we would get through this…. eventually.

I'm sorry to tell you that if you suffer with the same feelings, there doesn't seem to be a magic cure! I tried loads of things, swaddling, swinging, rocking, singing, white noise, holding them in weird ways suggested online, dancing with them while wearing a red sock on one hand and a pair of ear muffs over my head singing 'Donald Where's Your Troosers', but nothing worked… it was just going to take time!

It really sucks to hear that when you are only up to week four, but by around three and a half months my baby's screams became a lot less frequent. The early evening screaming stopped and the mental hell torture started to ease off and the days became more bearable. I also started to enjoy my tea again!

You will feel a lot of frustration when you go through the 'crying' stage, the fear you feel at their every wail. The worry that something is wrong with them and the dread that they will never stop.

This can be a time when you can feel a lot of anger and irritation towards them when they start screaming and will not stop. Health professionals recommend you don't leave your baby alone for the first 6 months, but when the crying was too much for me, I found leaving them safe in their cot and taking 5 minutes in another room to compose myself and take a breath, really helped me to stay calm and patient. You are going through major sleep deprivation and continuous screaming is not going to make it any easier. Do not be afraid to ask for help, what you are feeling will be exactly the same as probably nearly every other mother and father at some point.

I once searched online for - 'Why do I feel angry towards my baby when he cries?' and was surprised but also very comforted and relieved by the fact that it was a completely normal reaction, a lot of mums felt the same way I did. A baby's screams are designed to get your heart racing, your blood pumping, your emotions heightened and if you're exposed to a lot of screaming and hardly any sleep it is completely understandable that you'll feel frustrated at times when you are going through this stage in your child's development.

It may also seem like everyone else's baby never seems to cry as much as yours does. You will be out at playgroups or on play dates and your little one kicks off every time, yet all the other babies are perfectly content and calm fast asleep in their buggies. You may start to feel like you don't want to leave the house in case a screaming episode occurs and you can't stop it. Again, it is that feeling of not being able to control the situation which starts to freak you out.

Start talking about it to other people, and once you do you will soon realise that everyone feels the same way. You are all struggling with more or less the same issues and it really will make you feel better when you realise it is not just you that's going through this. I remember feeling so relieved when my sister told me that she had often felt so frustrated and angry with her girl's screams, she had to leave her in the conservatory and go in the garden sometimes so she could get away from hearing her for a few minutes, to compose herself and shout a few expletives into the air.

On top of the baby crying, there are also your tears. They will come, oh yes they will come and probably a lot in that first three to four months. With my first baby, I cried at least once a week for the first ten weeks. Why? There are many reasons…

Tiredness

Frustration

Guilt

Hormones

Jealousy

Anger

Feeling a failure

Worrying too much

A Save the Children advert

For no reason

It's another normal part of becoming a first time mother, your whole life as you knew it has completely changed and you are coming to terms with your new life and the responsibility of a tiny baby 24/7. Your friendships, your finances, your emotions, your family, have all changed and I think it would be more strange not to have the odd sob now and again.

Think of it as a release, all that emotion having somewhere to go and I know I always felt a bit better after letting it all out in a massive sobbing episode. I remember being on a play date with my friend who also had a baby the same time as me and both our little ones were screaming their heads off and we both just looked at each other and started crying along with them and all four of us were in hysterical crying mode! Then we just paused, looked at the hilarious scene, and burst out laughing - and couldn't stop!

This time will pass and you will get through it, know that for sure!

Chapter Five

SLEEP (OR LACK OF IT)

Just five more minutes!

You will have no doubt been told by numerous people about the sleepless nights you will have once your baby is born. Are you prepared for it?

Er, no!

It will be like nothing you have ever experienced before, and will perhaps be the most evil thing you encounter during the early days of parenthood (And you thought the clown from 'IT' was scary!)

You may have had a few big nights out in times gone by, where you have stayed up all night dancing, living it up, and coped just fine without any sleep. You may be thinking it won't be so bad, as you are used to only getting a few hours sleep a night.

Trust me, it will be that bad… and a whole lot worse!

I never realised how important sleep was to the human body until I stopped getting any! It affects your mental health, physical health, quality of life and safety (if you don't believe that, search online and you will be surprised).

So these first few months are going to be very tough indeed, and you will feel and experience a lot of crazy things. Do not lose all hope, hold on, because it will get better….

When the lack of sleep starts to kick in around four to ten weeks you may start to feel:-

Like your head is a bowling ball

Snappy and irritated by just about everything and everyone

Total lack of libido

Feeling low and depressed

Wanting to eat more 'fatty' foods

Low energy

Physically sick

Confused and disorientated

Low concentration

Forgetful

Teary

Envious feelings towards your baby who is sleeping

Envious feelings towards your partner who is sleeping

Envious feelings towards anyone who is sleeping (The cat? The dog?)

Fear and dread of going to bed knowing that you will be up half the night

Wishing for your old life where sleep was a part of it

Worry that your sleep will never recover

Resentful towards the baby for taking away your right to sleep

I was surprised just how alike the symptoms were for both conditions when I looked on the internet about post natal depression and sleep deprivation.

My mind and my body were affected hugely by sleep deprivation. I used to love going to bed at night, then after having a baby I started to dread it. I would go to bed madly planning in my head what sleep I would be hoping to get - 'Right, if I get to bed at 8pm, fall asleep by 8.45, that gives me about 2.5 hours of sleep until I have to be up to feed baby. Then if I fall back to sleep by 12.30 that gives me 2 hours before I have to be up again blah blah blah'. And of course it is never as you plan it, as you don't factor in your partner snoring! Or the fact you can't get off to sleep because you are worrying about your child when they are in Year Seven, getting bullied by a rough boy and how you will handle it?!

You start to almost obsess about sleep, and then that in itself makes it harder, because your mind is whirring all the time! It will not help if you are around other mums who proudly declare their babies are sleeping through at four weeks and you'll just want to slap them (the mums not the babies - lol)!

You will also, at some point, swear under your breath in the middle of the night, when you hear your baby start to cry. We have all done it, you are enjoying your sleep, no doubt dreaming of the future when you can actually get four continuous hours of non-stop slumber, then you'll hear a distant sound like whimpering in the distance, which turns to full blown screaming! You'll open your eyes startled and wide awake quickly realising that sleep time is over and that you have to get up and feed a baby. 'For *ucks sake!'

You will also play the crying game with your partner, which is usually good fun. Both of you will quite clearly hear the baby crying, but both of you will lay stiff in bed, in the sleep position and perfectly still - not giving anything away, pretending to be fast asleep and oblivious until one of you cracks. It is such a great feeling to win at this game and then roll over when they get back into bed, saying 'Oh was that the baby?'

I am willing to bet that, at some point, a health professional will just tell you to 'sleep when the baby sleeps'; 'Catch up on your lost sleep during the day!' Ha! I love that one. It will never happen, sorry to tell you that.

You will find that sleep becomes a huge part of your day, everyone will ask you about it.

How much sleep did you get last night? And every day you'll recount what happened the night before, forever hoping that maybe, just maybe, tonight will be better.

Your own thoughts will be full of sleep related questions:-
When will I get some quality unbroken sleep again?
When will my baby sleep through the night?
Can I die from lack of sleep?
Will tonight be the night I get more than two hours?
Am I damaging my brain by not getting any sleep?
Will this lack of sleep now affect me in the future?

Every night you may go to bed full of hope and expectation that tonight will be the night you don't get woken up at 1am and 3am for bottles, or tonight will be the night you fall asleep quickly and feel more refreshed in the morning! You know what, one of those 'tonights' will be the night, so hang in there!

As soon as you start to get your sleep back, even if it's only three or four continuous hours you will feel so different in yourself. It will almost feel like a black cloud lifting and moving away from the top of your head. You will feel happier in yourself, you will feel happier towards the baby and your partner. You will have more energy and just be able to cope better with things, especially the cries of a baby. It all happens around the three to four month mark, you start to get your sleep back, and the baby starts crying less.

Your body is an amazing thing, it will cope, and it will get you through this horrific time, even when it feels all hope is lost you will find your sleep again - and it will feel like the greatest gift ever given to you in your whole entire life! In a former life you may have wished for fortune, jewels and to get into (or at least a thigh into) a size ten pair of jeans. You may find now, that after becoming a first time mum all your wishes are considerably more modest!

Chapter Six

BODY/SELF IMAGE

'I feel fat and ugly'

That was my first thought, upon staring at myself naked in the mirror after having a baby.

Why I felt the need to stand naked in front of the mirror, jiggling my wobbly tummy and saggy boobs about, while negatively scrutinising my stretch marks and saggy skin, I will never know! But will you do the same? Yes, probably! Why? Because we are women, and we beat ourselves up about absolutely everything! Even though we have just had a baby, we still can't give ourselves a break!!

It's like a form of self torture that we put ourselves through, we can't say 'relax you've just had a baby'! We feel the need to compare ourselves to everyone else in the entire world who has had a baby. So instead of feeling grateful that I still had a body after going through labour and child birth, some of my thoughts were...

My belly's all wobbly

My boobs look like Spaniel's ears

Jesus, look at all my stretch marks

My skin is loose

Where did all those rolls of fat come from?

How come I still can't see my fanny?

I look pale

My dark circles under my eyes look darker

My hair looks frizzy and lank
I look tired
I look like I've aged twenty years
I feel fat
I feel ugly

It doesn't help that I'm hearing on the telly all about how some model has lost all her baby weight in four weeks and is already back in her size ten skinny jeans and isn't she wonderful and doesn't she look great, blah blah blah.

Hang on a minute, surely you're not going to compare yourself to a Supermodel, who is married to a multi-millionaire, who has a nanny, a personal chef, a personal trainer, a gym at home, a swimming pool and a size eight body before she got pregnant?!

OH HELL YES, YOU ARE!

So already we're setting ourselves up for failure! It would be like comparing cheese with a car tyre, but we still do it.

We all know it is completely normal to feel a bit down about the changes that happen to your body during pregnancy and after birth, but it can still be tough coming to terms with them. Plus, the guilt you then feel for dwelling on body issues when you've got a beautiful healthy baby to care for and you beat yourself up constantly about being 'selfish' and 'vain' for worrying about how you look.

A few things you might feel:-
Shocked at how much weight you gained
Self conscious in your clothes
Worried you'll never lose all the weight you put on
Not wanting your partner to see your naked body
Fed up with the military precision still needed to shave your pubic hair
Feeling like your partner won't find you attractive any more
Embarrassed by your body shape

Upset about how your stomach looks

Down about having to buy some bigger sized clothes, as none of your old clothes fit

Feeling low/teary about how you look

Upset over the saggy boobs and skin

Feeling unable to accept your changing body

Guilty for feeling bad about yourself when you have a baby to look after

Worried about how your vagina will feel (bucket?)

What will my vagina look like, will it be all mashed up?

Will I ever be able to cough or sneeze without crossing my legs again?

I think some people are lucky and their bodies do not change all that much during pregnancy, so hopefully you will be one of them. Unfortunately for me, I was eating lots of cake so I wasn't one of the 'lucky' ones.

After my babies, I found myself sub-consciously hiding my belly with my arm or a cushion or the baby and when it came to getting undressed in front of my partner - eek! Forget about it! I'd try every trick in the book, so he wouldn't see my wobbly bits in all their unfiltered glory! Why? I'm sure he wouldn't have cared one bit that my tummy was like a tub of jelly - if I'd actually asked him.

You may find yourself for the first few months walking around in baggy clothes not having time to do your make up or hair, as it's all about the baby, and it is the baby that gets all of your time and energy. We tend to put ourselves way down on the priority list and that's just how it is.

If you do get half an hour to yourself when your baby is asleep it is usually those times when you are rushing around like a whirlwind, thinking right now is the time to clean the bathroom, put a wash on, do the washing up, hang the clothes on the line, sort out tonight's tea, clean the baby sick off my trousers, put the dishes away.... it really is amazing how much you can get done in half an hour (before children I'd probably have just gone to the toilet in that time). Although I am sure painting your nails and straightening your hair will not be on your priority list in that precious time when your baby sleeps.

It will sometimes feel like you are just 'functioning' in those early months, you may be feeling like a slave to the baby, you are there to dress him, feed him, change his nappies, get him to sleep, entertain and so on. Time for yourself is just on the back seat for a while. Some people will tell you - 'well, it took nine months for your body to get to that shape so it will take at least another nine months for you to get back to how you were before.' Other people may tell you - 'God, have you got another baby in there?' Try not to let other people's comments get to you too much and make you feel down. A lot of the time they are trying to encourage you, but sometimes it just comes out wrong. Yes, thank you Dad, that is your 'Get yourself down the gym and lose that belly' comment.

I decided that, instead of beating myself up about how I looked after pregnancy and negatively listing things in my mind of all the things I hate about my body, I thought no! I'm going to flip it round and only think of the positive things - and it really does help lift you.

I'm alive

I've got my own teeth

My baby is fit and healthy

I'm so lucky to be a mother

I don't have halitosis

My body is amazing, it grew a human!

I will lose the baby weight when I'm ready

Two hearts have beaten inside me

Stretch marks will fade

I can lay on my belly now

Be grateful and thankful for what I've got and not what I haven't

I've given my partner his first born child - no-one else can ever do that

My boobs will look better with time - and failing that there are good bras out there

If I look in the mirror, take my glasses off and squint, I have the body of Cindy Crawford!

It is so true what they say, that a positive thought is much stronger than a negative one - so if you do start feeling down or low about the way you look after having a baby, try to spin it around in your mind into something positive and start to think about the things you do like about your body and so on. You just gave your baby life, so come on you are pretty amazing!

Chapter Seven

SEX/COMMUNICATION WITH PARTNER

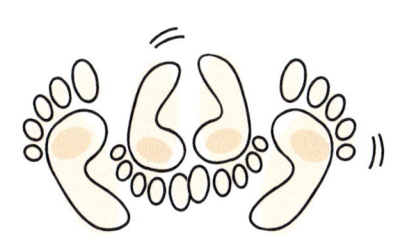

'I'm never having sex again'

That could be one of your first thoughts when this subject creeps into your mind after having your first baby. This thought could continue to be your only thought for quite a few months after having your baby.

From the many conversations I have had about this subject with my friends and topics on daytime tv shows etc be reassured it is completely normal to go off sex and it is nothing to stress about.

To me it felt like having sex was something I wanted to do about as much as I wanted to re-train and become a night nanny for newborns!

Just look on the internet under 'Why do woman go off sex after they have a baby' and there will be hundreds, if not thousands, of articles about it.

After having a baby, your thoughts are all over the place, and if sex is mentioned there might be a few reasons why you are just not interested.

You're just too exhausted

You have had a baby all over your body all day I just do not want to be touched

It is too soon, I don't feel ready

You feel too self-conscious of your post baby figure - worrying about sagging skin, droopy boobs, stretch marks and extra pounds

You may still be coming to terms with the trauma of the birth

You don't feel physically ready

You feel scared, in case the sex will hurt

Petrified of getting pregnant again

Nervous of how your vagina will feel to your partner after a baby has passed through it (like throwing a welly up the high street?)

Worried if your partner will still find you attractive

Scared that the baby will wake up

Not wanting to 'do it' with the baby in the room

Just not feeling remotely sexy

Anxious that sex will eat into your 'sleep' time

Embarrassed about how you look naked

Find your partners advances irritating and want to shrug off affection

All of the above is completely normal (I know because I saw a sex therapist on a daytime show talking about it), after having a baby your libido is practically non-existent because your body knows it needs to save all the energy for looking after your baby. It is a completely natural thing that sex will fade for a little while. Don't panic too much though, because in time it will return and if it doesn't there are plenty of places you can get help and advice from about it. Be aware though it is not a quick thing, some experts say it can be anywhere between six months and two years before your libido returns.

I think the biggest thing is to perhaps reassure your partner about why you do not want to have sex. They may be struggling with their own insecurities. They have just become a father and are dealing with a whole host of emotions themselves, so constant rejection if not explained can make them think its them - that they are the reason you do not want to have sex because you are not attracted to them any more.

I think in this circumstance it is okay to say those immortal words 'It's not you, it's me'. Reassure them that you do still find them attractive and that sex will be back on the agenda in the future, but at the moment you are just not there yet - because out of all the reasons for you not wanting sex it's definitely NOT because you suddenly don't find your partner attractive any more! But maybe they need to hear that from you?

However, saying all that, we can be our own worst enemy sometimes for thinking that our partners think like we do - we are worrying about extra pounds, saggy skin and droopy boobs and our self-esteem is a bit low, so we're quite negative and hard on ourselves, so maybe our partners are thinking the exact opposite!

Mmmmmm Boobs !!!

Sex is just low, low, very low on the list of things you want to be doing after having a baby. You're exhausted from looking after a newborn all day and being up all night. Our beds become sacred places where we worship at the sleep temple. They are no longer places where we think about sex, or anything remotely to do with sex.

Yes of course it will change, you will want to have sex again but it is going to take time. Hey you may even be completely opposite, and become a right randy old bugger!

What is it people say…. having a baby brings you closer together?

PAAAAH!!! BLURGH!!!

Imagine a large old oak tree in the middle of a forest. The trunk is thick and sturdy, the roots are strong and deeply buried into the earth. It has lasted for hundreds of years, weathered through the worst storms history has thrown at it and it's still standing….

Then it gives birth to a newborn!

Argh! Those roots and foundations are shaken like never before. Every part of that tree is tested to its absolute limit, it's teetering on the brink of being ripped apart?!

(Okay, that may be a bit too dramatic!)

But you get the picture, having a baby will be a huge strain and test on your relationship, and as long as you work together and work as a team and keep communicating with each other - you will survive!

When you are in the 'baby bubble', which is probably the first two to three weeks, you will lovingly look into each other's eyes and say things like 'We created our baby', 'We did that!' and 'I love you' with lots of cuddles holding your beautiful newborn baby in-between you - calling each other 'mummy' and daddy'. Yet after that, when the sleep deprivation hits and the screaming starts, you find yourself snapping and feeling irritated with each other at the smallest of things. And this is why staying positive and talking to each other is key, because things could really take a nasty turn if we totally lost sight of each others feelings and emotions.

They say to try and create a team feeling with your little family, you're a team and you stick together. When one is feeling down, you help lift them up, when one is feeling tired you let them rest, get through problems together and keep the team spirit alive (alcohol and chocolate can help with this). If you do support each other through this early start of parenthood, I think you will become a lot closer for it.

The saying that a problem shared is a problem halved is so true and we would all definitely benefit from being more open about things to everyone, and not just our partners - there are other family members, friends, colleagues etc., because along with all the highs that come from having a baby, there can be a lot of lows too - and when you can talk to people about things openly and honestly, it can sometimes be a huge weight off your chest.

I know it's sometimes hard to talk to the people we are closest to about our innermost thoughts, fears and worries. It could be due to:-

Not wanting to worry them

You don't want them to think you can't cope

You might be worried about their reaction to what you tell them

Worried they might think you are a failure, or a bad mum

Frightened if you start talking you won't stop

I do think we put way too much pressure on ourselves to be 'perfect' and it's just trying to live up to something that doesn't exist and doesn't need to exist. Everyone is struggling with something or other at different times in their lives and when we do start talking to each other about this sort of stuff we realise that we are not alone, that we can get help and help others just by being honest and talking.

Another hurdle to face can be when your partner has to return to work after paternity leave.

The feeling of sheer panic, fear and dread!

How will you cope on your own? You are going to be solely responsible for your baby's life!

It can sometimes be quite daunting and scary and it will be totally normal to have some worries and fears about this time.

You will be fine though! The thought of something can sometimes be a lot more terrifying than the actual reality. You will cope, you will find your new routine, so do not panic too much.

However, when your partner has returned to work after a while, and you have been at home on your own with the baby for a few weeks, you may find your thoughts towards your partner can be negative.

Resentful towards him for being able to leave the house

Resentful that he has his life back and yours has turned upside down, living as a baby slave all day

Envious that he gets independence back all day

Feeling snappy and irritated towards him

Feeling like they don't understand what you are dealing with on a day to day basis

Not telling your partner if you have had a bad day

Feeling like you want to slap him in the face when he comes home all jolly and asks how your day went (after you've had the day from hell)

Putting a brave face on everything and saying 'all fine'

Clock watching until they're home

Feeling lonely

Feeling guilty about resenting your partner for going to work

Feeling guilty about not enjoying being at home all day with the baby

I think these feelings are pretty normal and it's like everything else, as time passes and you start to get your sleep back and the screaming dies down a bit, you don't feel these negative thoughts any more - and you start to enjoy things, becoming a lot more positive.

So, although you will find in these early months it is difficult to communicate with your partner, try to work together and don't push each other too far away and then struggle to find your way back. If you can't talk, I find an email is a good idea, as you can get all your feelings out without being interrupted and it is a bit therapeutic, like writing in a diary. Also, your partner has time to digest it, whilst being outside of the house environment - so when they do come home you can both talk about it, without it being so raw.

It was only when I looked back after having my babies, and actually talked at length to my partner about our times with newborns, that I realised a lot of the feelings and worries I was experiencing and fretting about were feelings that he shared. If I had talked more to him while I was going through it, it would have really helped with making us feel even more like we were in this together, and we were a team. We would get through it and connect even more because of the experiences we have shared.

Chapter Eight

COMPARING YOURSELF WITH OTHERS AND GOING OUT

'Everyone else is doing it better'

That is a thought that will no doubt come into your brain at some point during the first six months of motherhood.

You'll possibly think:-

Everyone is coping better than me

They all seem like naturals

Everyone else's baby seems to be sleeping through the night

They all seem to be really enjoying motherhood

They look great, I look shit

I feel inadequate next to them

Feeling inferior when their babies are all crawling and yours hasn't even rolled over

Guilty because they are all going to baby classes and you are not

Guilty if they are all breastfeeding and you take out your bottle

They are all back in their normal clothes and you are still in your maternity jeans

Their babies never seem to cry

Toy envy! She has much better toys than I do

Change bag envy! She has a much better change bag than I do

Pram envy! She has a much better pram than I do

It's a crazy world but when you become a mum and you start 'hanging' out with other mums, all sorts of silly thoughts can take over your mind. You would think that being around other new mums would make you feel more at ease, but unless they are close friends it can sometimes feel like you are being judged by everyone - from how you feed your baby, to how you sing 'incy wincy spider' at playgroup.

You will no doubt find that simple things like leaving the house, which before babies was a simple task of just walking out the door, has turned into a military operation. There is no 'nipping' or 'popping' out any more when babies are in the mix.

You will also, at some point, have every intention of going out to that baby class or play date - but after the stressful morning of projectile vomit, the green runny poo and the screaming fit you will inevitably say 'F**k it!' and text them to say you are both ill!

If you do happen to make it out of the house, it can also be stressful managing a baby in various places like baby classes, supermarkets, cafés etc. Your adorable child may decide today is the day they will just scream and scream and scream for no apparent reason, other than they can… you just feel everyone's eyes upon you and their disapproving stares, which can make you feel very self-conscious and uncomfortable.

It will not help either if you're surrounded by your 'new mum' friends and they all gush about how wonderful their babies are all the time and how in love they are with them, how their lives are perfect now, that they don't actually talk about the other side of things, about the hard times, and the struggles, as you could find yourself sitting there praying someone will just say - ' Actually, I feel like it's a bit shit looking after a baby sometimes'.

You may find that you have to be the one that says it, and once you do they all breathe a sigh of relief and say 'thank god you said that, because I have felt like that too!' I know nearly all my friends who have had babies have all agreed that it's definitely a bit shit sometimes looking after a baby, so we can't all be the only ones that think it -can we?!

Do not put yourself under any pressure to go to baby groups or meet lots of new mums, if there are ones you like then great, but if not then that's fine too. Let's face it your baby won't have any memory of anything until they're about four anyway, so they are not going to hold it against you that you didn't take them to some active fit bean bag bounce pan pipes music soft play group at the local community centre when they were three months old!

You will find it hard not to compare your baby to other people's and not look on the internet to see what a four month old baby should be doing - we have all done it. The key is not to obsess about it (ha! Good luck with that one), your baby really will do it when they are ready, and don't think everyone else is doing it better than you, because they are not. Everyone is just doing the best they can, just like you.

Chapter Nine

GUILT AND WORRY

Guilt and Worry your two new best friends

Unfortunately your new mates are crap friends and really, really suck!

Over the course of the six months since having a baby, you will hang out with your two new best friends probably on an hourly, daily, or certainly weekly basis.

You will hang out with GUILT over a few things like:-

Not wanting sex

Shouting at the baby

Feeling resentful towards the baby

Leaving baby with partner or family for more than five minutes

For feeling irritated or angry towards the baby

For not showing your partner more affection

For not contacting or seeing your friends as much

Not feeling happier

Not losing any baby weight

Not breastfeeding

Not bathing the baby every day

Not taking baby to that swim class each week

Not talking to your partner about how you're feeling about things

For having any negative feelings towards the baby, when so many people would wish to be in your position

For not coping as well as others seem to be

For sometimes wishing for your old life back

For resenting your partner for getting to go to work and having a break

For wanting to return to work

Feeling snappy and irritable towards partner

For not feeling totally 'in love' with your baby from the second they were born

Guilty for being too long in the shower

GUILT…...GUILT….GUILT

Then you will get to spend time with WORRY:-

Worrying about suddenly dying

Worrying about baby suddenly dying

Worrying about partner suddenly dying

Worrying about anyone suddenly dying

Worrying about how your partner feels about not having much, or any, sex

Worrying about how your partner is coping with being a father

Worrying about baby choking or getting ill

Worrying you'll never lose weight

Worrying about your vagina

Worried you're not going to be able to cope with motherhood

Worrying you're not going to bond with the baby

Worrying you're doing things wrong

Worrying you'll never get any sleep again

Worrying about the baby's temperature

Worrying about family and friend dynamics changing

Worrying about when your baby is fifteen and what options they will take for GCSE

WORRY…...WORRY…..WORRY

Whether it is worse now because of social media and the fact that we have access to snippets of so many peoples lives, we can see what they are doing, where they are going, what they had for lunch, who they are with, what they bought from the gift shop and we start to feel guilty that our children are missing out? That they seem to be raising their babies better than we are? Or is it all just bollocks?

Truth be told, probably all the guilt you feel will purely be in your own head. Your partner, your family and your friends will not be thinking any of the things you'll expect them to think. It's just another case of beating yourself up and putting too much pressure on yourself, because that's just what we do.

And the worry? Well sorry, I'm reliably informed (by my mother) that worry is with you for life! Doesn't matter if your baby is three months or thirty years old they are going to worry the life out of you, as I'm sure you do your mother?!

The guilt and the worry was something that also took me by surprise after having children. I was quite a carefree person before, and never really worried about that much, but literally as soon as my baby popped out then.... oh my God! I turned into Mrs Worry Wart and really had to get myself in check to ensure my thoughts didn't send me crazy.

We're not sterilising right!

We're not warming the bottles right!

We're not mixing them correctly!

We didn't sterilise that dummy after he dropped it!

Does he have a milk allergy?

Does he have colic?

Does he have reflux?

Is he teething?

Is he developing normally?

Is our washing powder okay?

Why is his poo green?

Have we done something to make his poo turn green?

He's not rolling over yet, is there something wrong?

Then, after all these crazy frantic ravings about four months into it, I saw a programme where babies are basically drinking stale water from a puddle, down a dirt track, that a baboon just weed into and I thought hang on! I am sitting here worrying about whether I'm going to make my baby ill because his dummy fell out and landed on my carpet and I put it straight back into his mouth, without putting it in a cup with boiling water for five minutes first?! Get a grip woman! Babies are tough little buggers! What do they do in outer Mongolia?! So I really started to chill out - and it made a huge difference.

My advice to you would be – yes, you will feel guilty about anything and everything, (my sister calls it mother's guilt) and yes you will worry about anything and everything, but do not let it take over your brain. After a few seconds, just turn it on its head and say 'no', everything will be fine, we are all okay - and shut it down, before it has a chance to get really out of hand.

This whole mindfulness attitude that is everywhere now is definitely one to adopt when you feel your thoughts running away from you. Just stop, take a minute, breathe, think about where you are, what you are doing at that particular time and shift the focus from your mind and the thoughts that are racing around, to your body and what you can feel. Failing that, a good sing song at the top of your voice can shake yourself out of being lost in your mind. I'm loving 'My Favourite Things', 'Climb Every Mountain', 'Do-Re-Mi' from 'The Sound of Music', and the theme tune from 'Poddington Peas' at the moment.

Another thing to remember is that everyone else is going through the same guilt and worry that you are too, you are by no means alone. Just ask your partner.

Chapter Ten

SEE THE FUNNY SIDE

Laugh until you wet yourself
(which will not take long after having a baby)

The one thing becoming a parent has taught me is you have definitely got to see the funny side. You will face so many things that will make you want to cry, scream, run for the hills, question your sanity! But you will also have the biggest belly laughs over the craziest things too. Nothing will beat a good laugh and giggle even when you're feeling sad and low.

Have you ever tried pretend laughing? I have. I read that the brain cannot determine a real laugh from a fake one, so when you do it the brain releases the happy hormones just the same and it's supposed to give you the same high as real laughing does.

Try it now!
Just laugh out loud! I dare you! Start laughing hysterically!
Do you feel better?

Sometimes I did this when my baby was screaming his head off and wouldn't stop and I felt like I was about to burst into tears too, I just started laughing really loudly and wildly instead. Then the reaction on my baby's face made me laugh for real and I just got the giggles and could not stop. Unfortunately, I think I weed myself a little bit after that.

You will have lots of things that will make you smile over the next six months.

The way you will obsess over what change bag to buy, trawling the internet to find the perfect one and spending way more than you really wanted to. Then, once the baby is here after about a month of faffing around with the one you paid for, you will just use the free one from 'Boots' all the time.

You will do exactly the same with a pram, reading reviews on each pram you find and trying to wander round the few shops that actually sell prams now, trying to pick out the perfect one. Then, after a while, you will end up just using that cheap stroller you got from the supermarket 90% of the time, and that big travel system you bought will just collect dust in the dining room corner.

You will no doubt be eager to take your baby swimming, full of excitement about seeing how they react to being plunged into the pool, (for the whole ten minutes they're in there for) and then you will never go again for about six months because it was such a faff to get both of you ready and in the pool, then out the pool getting dressed with a screaming baby in tow.

You will also put your name down for different classes to take your baby to, but then realise that you just cannot get up, get dressed, get baby dressed, have breakfast, pack bags, and sort out the pram in time for that 9.30 start!

You will hate putting coats on babies

You will curse at socks that never stay on babies' feet

Car seats will become your arch enemy

You will wash poo covered baby vests for the first few times then think…. sod this! Get the scissors out, cut it off baby and chuck it!

You will buy little cute baby shoes and booties that they will never wear

Those cute dungarees you bought will never be worn because they are a nightmare to get baby in and out of

You will search online for pictures of baby poo

You will buy a rain cover for your pram and never use it

You will buy a sun shield umbrella for your pram which will never stay up

Your partner will ask you to try and squirt breast milk into his mouth

You will accidentally squirt breast milk into your baby's face

Your boobs will leak at other peoples crying babies

You will buy a cabbage for the first time in your life

You won't be able to sneeze or cough without crossing your legs for the foreseeable future

You will at some point drop their dummy and give it a quick suck yourself before putting it straight back into their mouth

You will use cotton wool and water on your baby's bum about once before you reach for wipes

You will pretend you did not smell anything when you leave a poo for your partner to change and just nip to the shop

Web search engines will become your permanent 'go to' sites. You may find yourself asking any or all of the following:-

Can you die from lack of sleep?

Why won't my baby stop screaming?

How much is a night nanny?

Why do babies projectile vomit?

Is green poo normal?

When do babies stop having wind?

Tips for helping wind?

Why does my baby scream in the early evening for no reason?

Can boobs get less saggy after time?

Will I ever want sex again after having a baby?

Do spiders have ears?

Whatever you do, try to keep that smile on your face and try and see the funny side - you just can't beat a good old belly laugh.

CONCLUSION

So, my dearest friend, answering your question about what it is like to have a baby and be a first time mum, you will find that you will be pushed to your absolute limits, you will feel and experience things that you could never have imagined. You will cry a lot of tears, some will be happy and some will be sad. You will be up and you will be down, you will have incredible highs - and sometimes incredible lows. Your emotions will feel like grains of sand that you can never quite get hold of and your patience will be tested beyond belief. You will have days where you want to drop to your knees and scream 'ENOUGH!'

Then you get closer to that six-twelve months……

You are falling in love with your beautiful gorgeous baby more and more as each day passes. Your bond is growing stronger and stronger. They sick on you, they poo on you, they scream at you, they keep you up all night long but then they give you the cheekiest, cheesiest one toothed grin and they give out the most amazing sound you will ever hear, a heart stopping chuckle and giggle and suddenly…….

ITS ALL FORGOTTEN!

I'M SO IN LOVE WITH MY BABY!

Good luck on your journey my friend. Don't ever forget you have an army of support standing shoulder to shoulder with you, so do not be afraid to ask for help.

P.S. You just know in another few months you will be telling everyone…. 'My baby was so good', 'He never cried you know!' and asking your partner 'Shall we have another one?' and 'It wasn't that bad was it?'

P.P.S Prepare yourself…… baby number 2 is coming? ……...

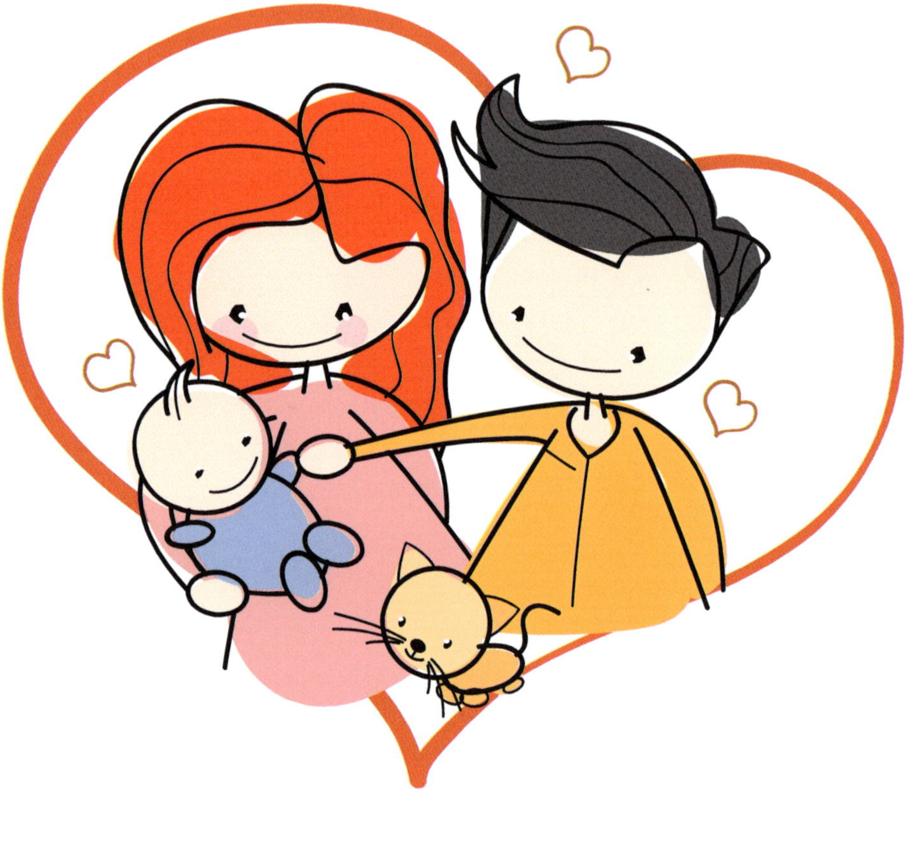

A FINAL THOUGHT

What did Dad think?

After writing down some of the things that I felt and thought when first thrust into the role of a first time mum, I thought it would be really interesting to ask my partner for his thoughts and feelings from when he also found himself in the same world, as a first time dad.

As, although we tried to talk to each other whilst going through it as best we could, we were at times like ships that passed in the night. Admittedly in those first six months we probably didn't spend enough time talking and listening to each other, as we were just functioning and spending most of our time listening to our beloved whirlwind first born son screaming from the top of his little lungs.

Preconceptions

Interestingly, he said exactly the same as me, that when he imagined himself to be a father he only thought of things like teaching them to ride a bike, doing D.I.Y, going out in the woods etc. He never once thought about the baby stage and late nights, bottles and crying.

He had not really been around many other people with babies, but on the occasions that he had, he only saw the positive fun side so he didn't feel as though he was prepared at all for the puking, being up all night, the screaming and not being able to see me so much. He also felt a burden financially, starting to worry more about the financial side of having a baby and how we would be able to afford the extra shopping.

Birth and coming home

His main worry was that he would be at work when it happened and that he would miss the birth. He wanted to be there but was nervous about the protocol - what he should do, where he should be? As he put it - 'Do I go top end or bottom end?'

When the baby was born, he did not feel instant love he just felt total relief it was over and me and the baby were okay. He felt nervous when he had to look after the baby on his own while I had a bath for twenty minutes, not daring to move in case he hurt him. It felt like the longest twenty minutes of his life! Worrying what to do if he started crying or had a poo (the baby not him).

First few weeks

Funnily enough he thought - 'What have we done?' and 'Am I ever going to enjoy a pint again?'. He said he researched many things and never felt very confident in what he was doing. He was looking forward to going back to work just to get away from the crying (the baby not me), and work started to feel a bit like a holiday from home. At the end of his working day, part of him would be looking forward to coming home to see me and the baby, but another part of him felt dread - knowing that the baby would be passed to him, and within ten minutes of being home he'd likely rather be at work because it was just so much to deal with in those first few months.

Crying

He felt totally unprepared for this part of becoming a father. He would feel angry with the baby when he wouldn't stop crying, finding himself swearing into thin air and even having to leave him a few minutes to regain composure. He felt there should be a reason for the screams, but there wasn't any and he found this particularly frustrating. He would start to dread the evenings because he knew that the early shift was his and listening to the crying and then having to get up in the night was hell.

Sleep

He was so tired that he didn't know how he drove himself to work. His emotions were all over the place due to sleep deprivation and he found himself being very quiet at work, grumpier towards people and not wanting to have conversations with anyone.

He said having a child made him feel a lot more emotional, and would find himself sometimes crying at random adverts on the telly, he felt up and down a lot of the time, mainly due to tiredness.

Body/Self image

He loved that my tummy was all jiggly like a water bed and wanted to just play with it for the first few days after I gave birth. He said he did not find me any less attractive, being bigger and more wobbly than I had been. He did wonder what sex would be like after a baby had travelled through my nether regions though!

Sex/Communication

He felt nervous about first having sex again, worried about possibly hurting me. He didn't feel at all bothered about having sex when the baby was asleep in his Moses basket next to the bed. He did feel a drop in his libido for the first few months and felt like he had no energy or stamina. However, sex was still on his mind a lot (surprise) and if I had been more up for it he would have definitely gone there.

He still felt able to talk to me as normal in those early months, but he did feel like he never saw me much, as I would head to bed not long after he got home from work, which I suppose in a way can make you feel slightly disconnected.

Guilt and Worry

He felt no guilt whatsoever when someone else was baby sitting for us such as parents, sisters etc. He just enjoyed the time away that we had together.

Worry, he noted, was something else. It came and went, but he would often find himself worrying about when the children were older. Worried about not being able to protect them when he was away from them.

All in all, being a dad has been the best thing he has ever done and he has no regrets and announces that 'it wasn't that bad was it, shall we have another one…?'

ARGH!!!!!!!!!!!!!!!!!!!!!!!!!!!!!!!!

Printed in Great Britain
by Amazon